W9-CBJ-749

The Red Cat Society

The Red Cat Society

Keeping Life Frisky, Fun, and Fabulous!

Created by Kevin Whitlark

Written by Patrick Regan

Andrews McMeel Publishing

Kansas City

The Red Cat Society

Text copyright © 2005 by Patrick Regan.

Illustrations copyright © 2005 Kevin Whitlark.

All rights reserved. Printed in China.

No part of this book may be used or reproduced in any manner whatsoever without written permission except in the case of reprints in the context of reviews.

For information, write Andrews McMeel Publishing, an Andrews McMeel Universal company,

4520 Main Street, Kansas City, Missouri 64111.

05 06 07 08 09 WKT 10 9 8 7 6 5 4 3 2 1

ISBN-13: 978-0-7407-5587-3

ISBN-10: 0-7407-5587-0

Library of Congress Control Number: 2005935654

The Red Cat Society

his all started innocently enough. Up until a few years ago, I was perfectly content with the luxurious life of a pampered house cat . . . sleep till noon, nibble a bit of kibble, let loose a token hiss at the dog, stretch, sleep, and repeat. Nothing to it.

But not too exciting, either.

Then one day, my human—a kind and generous woman who keeps my bowl filled and my fur well stroked—did something positively shocking. She came home one evening wearing a bright red feather boa. She was a walking cat toy! When I finally finished batting it around, I noticed that that wasn't the only change. She was also wearing a *très chic* red hat and—unless I'm as colorblind as a fourteen-year-old dog—a regal purple outfit. Even more obvious than the bold ensemble was the new spring in my human's step. Suddenly she was dancing through the house, laughing like mad on the phone, and acting like a little girl playing princess.

At first I was worried that she'd been sampling my catnip, but then one day a group of women came to the house wearing the same purple and red regalia, and I heard someone mention something called The Red Hat Society. I still wasn't sure what this society was all about, but it looked like more fun than a remnant sale at a yarn store.

Then one day between naps, it hit me. Why couldn't we tabbies start our own group dedicated to fun, friskiness, and feline friendship? The Red Cat Society was born!

Like the Red Hatters, we don't worry about rules, but we do have a few Guiding Principles:

- Fun is the ultimate purr-pose of life.
- Curiosity thrills the cat.
- Never underestimate the power of a positive cattitude.
- You've got nine lives—don't waste any of them.
- You *can* teach an old cat a new trick.
- Think outside the cat box.
- Do something every day that tickles your whiskers.
- Even if disagreements arise, ladies always keep their claws discreetly tucked away.
- No dogs allowed.

Well, the rest, as they say, is history. These days, you'll see Red Catters everywhere. This little book serves as a field guide to this fun-loving species. It will help to acquaint you with their whimsical ways, offer fashion tips for well-dressed cats, and—most importantly—reveal the many ways that Red Catters pack more fun into every day.

But first, a warning: The fab felines you'll meet in this book are *not* your average house cats. While Red Cats are not dangerous, they are unpredictable, outspoken, and occasionally outrageous. But most of all—like the women who inspired them—they are always ready to get out and play.

xxxooo,

Scarlet O'Haira

Founder and Exalted Queen Mother,
The Red Cat Society

Ah, the unbridled freedom and impetuousness of youth!

Aren't we glad we don't have to bother with *that* silliness anymore! Honey, we've finally reached the age when we can lay off the throttle, let out our tummies, and abandon once and for all that dream of freezing time at thirty-nine. To the youth-obsessed culture that tries to oppress us and undermine our esteem, let's bristle our fur and offer a hearty and spirited collective *hissss*.

And yes, I *will* nap in the afternoon so I can stay up late at night . . . and yes, I *do* still love to let my tail sway when I walk . . . and yes, I do reserve the right to have my say, live my way, and wear a red hat which doesn't suit me!

Youth is the gift of nature, but age is a work of art.

—GARSON KANIN

A grown woman should not have to masquerade as a girl in order to remain in the land of the living.

—GERMAINE GREER

Right on, Sister!

Red Cat Motto #1:

Fear No Age

Perhaps one has to be very old
before one learns to be amused
rather than shocked.

—PEARL S. BUCK

Red Cat Motto #2:

Laugh a Lot

(People will wonder what you're up to.)

Old age is
an excellent time for outrage.
My goal is to say or do
at least one outrageous thing every week.

—MAGGIE KUHN

A
ENLIGHTENED
THINKER AWARD
TO JAMES THURBER

I'm sixty-five . . . but if there were fifteen months in every year, I'd only be forty-eight. That's the trouble with us. We number everything. Take women, for example. I think they deserve to have more than twelve years between the ages of twenty-eight and forty.

—J.T.

At fifty, it's natural to look at our lives and start to ask some serious questions.

Where's the party?

Who does your hair?

What's for dessert?

Where did you get that gorgeous hat?

And most importantly . . .
What'll we do next?

TWENTY-NINE AND STILL HISSING

According to *Guinness World Records,* the oldest living cat is a Burmese called Kataleena Lady who lives in Melbourne, Australia. Kataleena Lady was born on March 11, 1977.

The purpose of life
is to fight maturity.

—DICK WERTHIMER

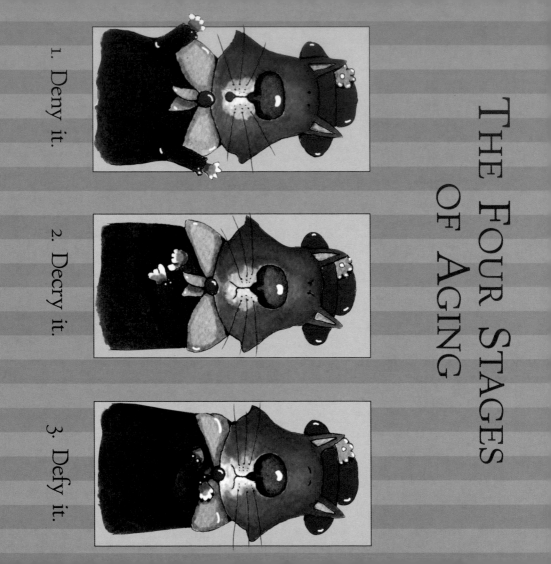

THE FOUR STAGES
OF AGING

1. Deny it.

2. Decry it.

3. Defy it.

4. Stand by it!

These colors
don't run.

(But they do sashay.)

Remember playing dress-up as kids? Pretending we were someone else—or an older version of ourselves? (Can you imagine?)

Well, in The Red Cat Society, we still play dress-up, but we don't do it to pretend we're someone else. We do it to proclaim loudly and proudly that we are us! When the purple and red come out, so do our true spirits.

"I hereby decree mandatory tea time in midafternoon with scones and real butter and sweet, sticky jams. I proclaim the right of all Red Cats to speak their mind, sing off-key, and dance without being asked. I banish all scales and two-piece swimsuits from the Red Cat Queendom . . ."

MEMBERS OF THE

ROYAL Red Cat COURT

Her Majesty, Queen Le Chat Rouge

Lady Naps-a-lot

Barroness de Brunch

MORE MEMBERS OF THE
ROYAL *Red Cat* COURT

Dame Whatadeal

Duchess of Drinks

Countess Me In

Princess Gabby, keeper of the royal gossip

Not a shred of evidence exists in favor of the idea that life is serious.

—BRENDAN GILL

Be open enough to try anything once.

Red Cat Motto #3:

Explain Nothing

Be who you are and say what you feel, because those who mind don't matter and those who matter don't mind.

—DR. SEUSS

Now that's a man who knew a few things about cats in hats.

Red Cat Vocabulary

Words every Red Catter should know

ESPRIT DE CORPS

THE COMMON SPIRIT EXISTING IN THE MEMBERS OF A GROUP AND INSPIRING ENTHUSIASM, DEVOTION, AND STRONG REGARD FOR THE HONOR OF THE GROUP.

"WITH THEIR SCARLET HEADWEAR AND UNMISTAKABLE ESPRIT DE CORPS, THE RED CATTERS WERE ADMIRED WHEREVER THEY WENT."

EBULLIENCE

THE QUALITY OF LIVELY OR ENTHUSIASTIC EXPRESSION OF THOUGHTS OR FEELINGS.

"THEIR EXCESSIVE EBULLIENCE NEARLY GOT THE RED CATTERS KICKED OUT OF THE RESTAURANT."

There is no pleasure
in having nothing to do;
the fun is in having lots to do
and not doing it.

—MARY WILSON LITTLE

Real Cat

CREED

Eventually to bed,

Sleep till you're done,

Keeps a girl frisky, friendly, and fun

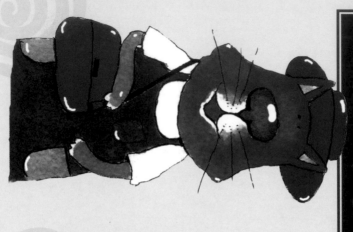

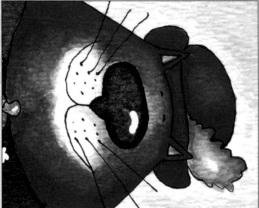

FOUR KEYS TO LIVING
THE Red Cat WAY

1. Never miss an opportunity to tell a sister how gorgeous she looks.

2. Learn to accept compliments gracefully.

3. Master the art
   of therapeutic loafing.

4. When in doubt,
   indulge.

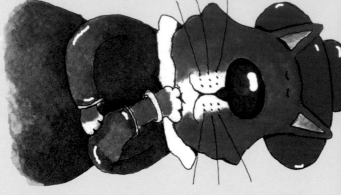

A Red Cat

AN ENLIGHTENED THINKER AWARD
TO OLIVER GOLDSMITH

They may talk of a comet, or a burning mountain, or some such bagatelle; but to me a modest woman, dressed out in all her finery, is the most tremendous object of the whole creation.

—O. G.

I think of life itself now as a wonderful play that I've written for myself, and so my purpose is to have the utmost fun playing my part.

—SHIRLEY MACLAINE

The problem with people who have no vices is that generally you can be pretty sure they're going to have some pretty annoying virtues.

—ELIZABETH TAYLOR

That's the voice of experience talking, honey.

Red Cat Motto #4:

Deny Your Age, But Not Your Appetites

Red Cat
WORKOUT TIPS

1. Start the day with stretches—your mind and your body.

2. Restrict lifting to eight ounces or less.

3. Work those cheek muscles—smile often.

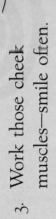

4. Keep motivation high—always work out with a group.

Laughter is inner jogging.

—NORMAN COUSINS

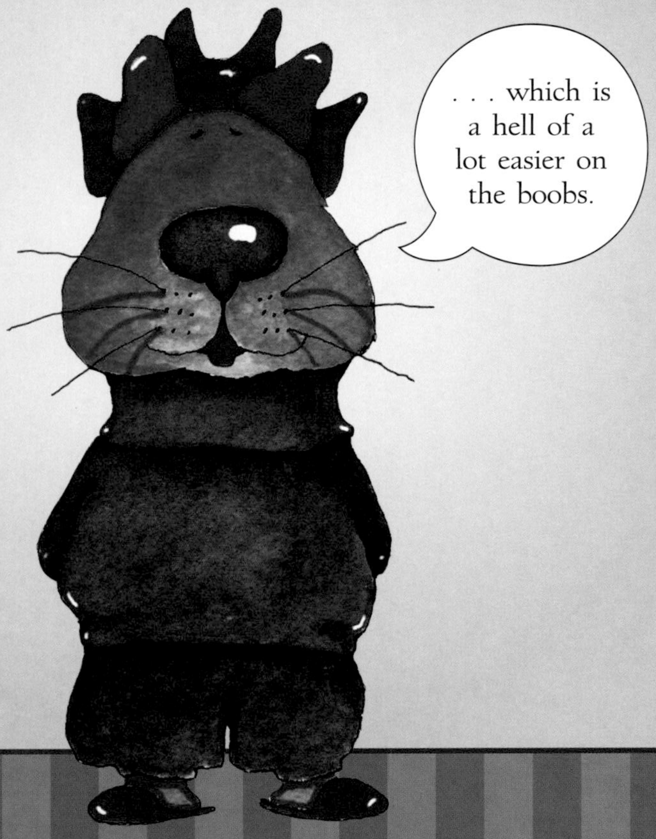

Red Cat Vocabulary

Words every Red Catter should know

VIVACIOUS

LIVELY IN TEMPER, CONDUCT, OR SPIRIT.

"VIVACIOUS RED CATS
ARE ALWAYS THE LIFE
OF THE PARTY."

CONVIVIAL

RELATING TO, OCCUPIED WITH, OR FOND OF
FEASTING, DRINKING, AND GOOD COMPANY.

"BEING CONVIVIAL IS FAR FROM TRIVIAL—
IT'S THE RED CAT WAY."

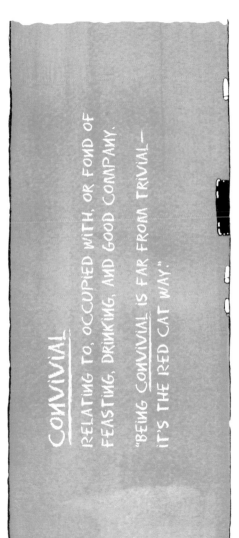

Red Cat

GEOMETRY POP QUIZ

Q. What's the lovliest distance between two points?

A.

A curve, darling.

WISDOM OF THE AGES

Humor is the only test of gravity, and gravity of humor.

—ARISTOTLE

Honey, when it comes to handling gravity, a sense of humor is a lot cheaper than a boob job.

further proof that we can handle anything nature throws at us.

Minnowpaws . . . .

I'm fine. *Just fine.*

Other than the hot flashes, cold flashes, night sweats, sudden bouts of uncontrollable crying, itchy skin, memory lapses, headaches, bodyaches, dizziness, bleeding gums, ringing ears, mysterious hair growth, and the fact that I sometimes pee when I sneeze . . . I'm just about friggin' perfect!

Well, it feels like cooking—it's actually hot flashes.

When men reach their sixties and retire they go to pieces.

Women just go right on cooking.

—GAIL SHEEHY

Red Cat Motto #5:

Cattitude Is Everything.

A positive attitude may not solve all your problems, but it will annoy enough people to make it worth the effort.

—HERM ALBRIGHT

Life is made up of many stages and not only are we always in one, we're always on one. At this midway point in life (yes, I plan a long, cantankerous run), I sometimes glance around the set and it hits me—this is the role of a lifetime! Damn the wrinkles and ditch the pancake make-up—I am ready for my close-up!

Red Cat Vocabulary

Words every Red Catter should know

PREEN

TO DRESS OR SMOOTH ONESELF UP; TO PRIDE OR CONGRATULATE ONESELF FOR ACHIEVEMENT; TO MAKE ONESELF SLEEK.

"WHEN YOU'RE A QUEEN, IT'S OKAY TO PREEN."

GRAND DAME

A USUALLY OLDER WOMAN OF GREAT
PRESTIGE OR ABILITY.

"ANYONE CAN BE AN OLD LADY, BUT IT TAKES
A RED CATTER TO BE A <u>GRAND DAME</u>."

WELCOME TO THE

Red Cat

NATION

We are everywhere!

California Calicos

Texas Tabbies

Back East Bluebloods

Southwest Senioritas

Canuck Kitties

FIVE GREAT THINGS ABOUT TURNING FIFTY

1. You save on heating bills during menopause.

2. You get plenty of exercise getting up to pee three times a night.

3. Damn the trends—no one expects fashion past fifty.

4. It's easier to embarrass your children and shock your neighbors.

5. Old women can get away with anything.

50 isn't fatal

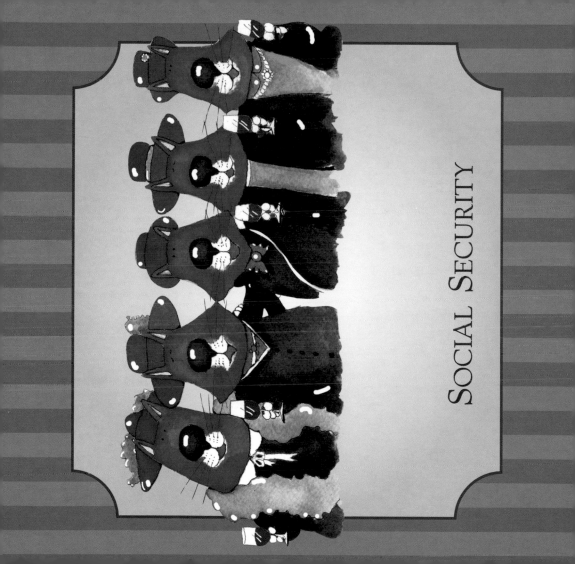

SOCIAL SECURITY

Look, I don't want to wax philosophic, but I will say that if you're alive you've got to flap your arms and legs, you've got to jump around a lot, for life is the very opposite of death, and therefore you must at very least think noisy and colorfully, or you're not alive.

—MEL BROOKS